Forget me Nots and Second Thoughts

KC Hannah

Presentation by *BookLeaf Publishing*

Web: www.bookleafpub.com

E-mail: info@bookleafpub.com

ISBN: 9789395890656

First edition 2023

*To the brightest stars in my sky; my family I
have and the family I chose.*

*Thank you for always believing in me, even
when I forget how to.*

ACKNOWLEDGEMENT

A huge thank you to everyone at Bookleaf Publishing for their support from start to finish in creating this and allowing a childhood dream to come true.

PREFACE

As a child I always knew I wanted to be an author and to have a book published that was mine and only mine. So when a friend, Kaley, sent me details of this competition, I couldn't not enter. Thus, a collection of poems from daily inspiration was born, and I'm forever grateful.

Cold Hands, Warm Heart.

It's easer to sit with the thoughts of what could
be, than to sit with the reality of what is.
The old sepia toned images of an idealistic past
is better company than the reality of what was.

Its easier to wrap your hands around a warm
mug when the weather is cold, than it is to cradle
the same mug on a hot summer day.
The temperature of the mug hasn't changed, the
contents made with the same repetitive instinct
as you've always had, you currently have and
you always will.

It is you, then, that has changed, are changing,
will change. It is you, dearheart, that has to learn
to sit comfortably with your technicolour past,
your 4k present and the storyboard of your
future.

It is you who must now embrace each reality,
memory and idea the same way you sit with that
mug on a cold winter day; seeking warmth,
seeking comfort, seeking peace.

Graceful in Defeat

Standing gracefully when you win is easy; when thousands have are cheering, when it's gone the right way, your way.

Standing gracefully in defeat, however, is something else entirely. When the cards are stacked against you and the chips are down, when you put your heart and soul into something only to watch it slip away and still be charming, poised and kind. That? That's a strength, your superpower. That's when you shine like you were supposed to. Doing the right thing isn't always easy, but neither is standing watching your world crumble around you with a soft smile on your face to hide the pain.

Being graceful in victory is beautiful, but there is nothing more hauntingly beautiful than being graceful in Defeat.

Grief

It isn't a destination, the lonely island of grief.
It is a daily commute- a must do thing - like
brushing your teeth or pouring a morning coffee
that will get you through the day.

Some days it's easier; a flying visit to the
memory of what once was, a smile and a laugh
and a fond farewell.

Other days, it's harder. There is a longing there
for arms that once held and once soothed, a
voice that once gave promises of happiness and
platitudes.

The length of the stay is determined by the
weather; whether the sun is bring enough to
outshine the pain or the rain is heavy enough
you use it to float.

When Heroes Fall

It's unrealistic to look at another human being and hold them to the highest of standards; to expect them to have all the answers, all do good always and be perfection personified. Its easy, though, when someone puts the starlight in your eyes to miss all the mistakes and the misgivings, to make excuses, to explain away any blemish or imperfection that is on them.

When the sunrises, and the moon disappears below the horizon, taking with it the light of a thousand shimmering stars, however, you're left with nothing but the reality and the bitter disappointment that the human you have held above all others is as broken, messy and fallible as you.

They were never supposed to be a mirror, your hero, they were supposed to be the hope and the promise of a better tomorrow, something to aspire to. So it is true then, that the disappointment belongs to you and you alone, for daring to believe that mere humans could dare to be better than they are.

Time

The sun sets, moon rises and at some point in history someone decided every 24 hours is a brand new day. Time is a construct used by many to decide how long things will last or have lasted and talk about it using many different measurements; minutes, moments, jiffy, eternity, years. We talk about timing flying by, rushing in, creeping past, how it stops. We discuss how finite it is, how we wish we had more.

We rarely talk about how time slows to a stop for some, while others go on with their lives despite there being a cataclysmic change in our notion of time. There is a definitive end to most things; a very obvious closure that can be felt across worlds, moments, lives. Sometimes, though, our worlds can be so in sync with each other but cataclysmic changes in one world doesn't change time in other people's worlds and that is where the difficulty lies.

Noone understands time as a concept when there are cataclysmic changes for some and not others; and sometimes, the only way to describe it is to liken it to those 6 days between Christmas and

New Year where time exists for noone, where there are no rules and noone tries to make it make sense. Until Midnight, and another 365 days of chaos and construct begins.

A Question of If

if you were guaranteed to get everything you
thought you would, by doing everything exactly
as you thought you should;
would I still receive your love in bouquets of
lillies and forget me nots,
or would I be discarded on the pile of could have
been without a second thought?

Last Dance

Endings don't always come with closure. Sometimes, they are nothing but misty eyed hugs on a crowded dance floor as the bells and bagpipes ring in another year of hopes and dreams.
There are times when the only closure you get is walking away knowing you've done your best.

Waiting, hoping and wishing for a different outcome only opens old wounds made long ago on another dance floor, with a different song playing.

Its time to pick your backing track, especially for the last dance.

Broken

To the girl in the mirror, I'm sorry I couldn't be a better friend and love you the way you needed to be loved.

I was busy fighting bloody wars in my own head that lasted for years. Some battles were harder than others, some took longer thanI hoped and those I lost I tried to remember that in the long run it was more important to win the war.

Its been too long since I last wrote a kind word to you that wasn't like a backhanded compliment. I need you to know that although I'm war weary and broken, I'm ready to come home and build the life we planned.

I just need you to be patient and remind me that although the world is vast and full of battles, that love will always guide us home.

I Won't

I won't allow those who wish to drag me down
dig their grip in so intensely that it numbs the
feeling and I no longer notice they're doing it
until I'm too far under to swim back out.

I won't allow those who choose to disrespect my
boundaries to dictate my life and my decisions,
my choices and things they know nothing about.

I won't listen to the voice that whisper "can't"
over and over every time I get my feet under me
and learn to stand on solid ground, they aren't on
my side, they're simply sowing seeds of doubt.

I won't allow myself to fall back on old ways
and means and coping mechanisms because it's
comfortable and familiar and safe. It's time to let
go, to change and to make things count.

Anyway

My mother once told me that life will knock you down. There is no if, it's an absolute certainty. Life will come along and sucker punch you when you're in the middle of laying down plans. So when it does, you have a choice. You can either stay there, and cry and hate the world as you watch it go by, or you can feel your feelings and get up anyway. You can get up and dust yourself off and keep on going, despite the pain. You can choose to live anyway, face the world anyway, get up and take another step anyway. Life doesn't hit and wait, it hits and continues along with the world. It happens anyway. Whether you're on the floor or not.

Courage has always been the harder choice. Getting up when you've been knocked down is always the harder choice. Sometimes, though, there is a beauty in the pain, in the brokenness, that you only see when change the perspective by getting up again and doing it anyway.

A Few Uncomfortable Truths

Being comfortable and feeling at home are wonderful until you become comfortable walking through broken glass and the chaos of raised voices because that is what home has come to mean. Home and all its familiar colours and sounds has fallen into chaos and when you open your eyes and really look around, you come to find that your comfortable, familiar landscape has changed and you can't remember when, how or why it changed.

It is then, in the midst of that storm, that chaos and the pile of broken pieces of a world that no longer exists, that you must release your hold and navigate your way to the exit. A change has already happened, there's nothing left for you here. It is time to find your new home and get comfortable being uncomfortable once again.

Things you never Said

She looks as though she wants to say something;
instead, she sighs,
looks at the floor and bites her lip, her fingers
twist and tangle together before she raises her
gaze,
and there, in here eyes,
is 1000 words and hopes and dreams and wishes
and I watch and wait, unable to do anything
as each of these things dies
and the lights go out behind her eyes, leaving a
dull, view of the broken world, reflected in her
gaze.
And as I turn and walk away, I know what she
was going to say, but still I cannot bring myself
to stay
in a space that was meant for me to keep.

Chaos

There's beauty in chaos, in failure,
in brokenness, in pain.
The tight grip of uncertainty,
in learning to breathe again.
The irrationality of emotion
and logic of reason,
the burning sting of anger,
the lack of choice, the forced hand
the changes of the season.
Everything doesn't have to be neat,
follow rules or make sense,
sometimes you have to break the mould
and choose yourself, because noone else will.

Humour Me

They say that if you don't laugh, you'll cry
and while I think that crying is okay
I can't spend my life in tears with red rimmed
eyes.

So each little broken piece of me adds to the
humour;
they hand me a giggle and a joke, a sarcastic
comment or flippant words that lift the mood
and get a more positive response from those
around me who watch with concerned eyes.

I don't hide my pain with humour, I use every
ounce of it in the humour and people think I'm
fine,
so we all carry on with the routine where I
continue to break and then make the jokes and
people continue to think I'm back to my old self.

I don't have the heart to tell them that there is no
difference anymore and every joke takes them
further from this truth.

Help

I find it easier to look fear in the eye when I'm
doing it for someone else.
To ask for something when it's not for me.
To accept help when it's on behalf of someone
else.

Its not that I am too proud or too stubborn to
ask.
It's simply down to the fact that I've never had
someone help without being asked the way I do
for others. I've never felt someone slip into the
role of helper the way I do for others; to see a
problem and to assume the helping hand role
before checking that it's okay with them that I
do.

I don't know how not to be strong, independent
and self sufficient because it is all I have ever
been, its all I've ever known.
So when someone finally asks if I need help the
answer will always be "no." Because I don't
need help. Sometimes, though, just sometimes I
would like it.

Little Voice

Its hard not to listen to the little voice inside
your head that whispers your flaws out loud; like
a sports commentator describing the who, what
and why as they watch it unfold.
The little voice that narrates every failing, every
mistake, loud and clear for everyone to hear,
hyping up the crowd and those at home, keeping
them on the edge of their seats.
That little voice who will, inevitably, find holes
in your performance and point them out despite
you doing so well and doing almost everything
right.
That Little Voice will leave you looking at a
victory like its broken, like its been handed to
you and not earned.
The thing you need to do in these moments, is
remind yourself, like most commentators, it has
its own agenda and it has nothing to do with
you.
Your best is, was and will always be louder than
that Little Voice.

Opposite

I'm not exactly a wall flower, but I'm also not the
prettiest in the room.
I'm not the one you eyes get drawn to across a
crowded space. I'm not the one who gets the
fairytale, gets the happily ever after, gets the
shoes, the dress and the Prince.
Girls like me aren't made for a crown, a fanfare,
a kingdom or gown.
But here's the thing.
Without girls like me rolling the dice and getting
the hand that says pressure and sacrifice;
There would be no fairytale, no handsome
Knight to save the damsel.
You see, in order for distressed dames to be
fortunate enough to sit around and be saved, the
rest of us have to save ourselves.
And be happy with our lot, as we gaze upon the
princess and everything we're not.

Never Break

Dear one, never let a bitter world keep you from
being the sunshine in a cloudy sky.
You could be the only Ray of light, of hope, of
warmth that makes someone get back up and
give life a try.
When the world tries to make you bend, break,
change and dim your shine;
firmly remind the world who they are dealing
with
that you are busy, to get a ticket and wait in line.
You have too many lives to save,
plans to make and rules to break,
To be anywhere less than where you are
changing the world with each choice you make.

A Letter to My Mother

I've missed you a million times in a thousand
ways
cried a week's worth of tears in a matter of days.
Picked up the phone to call you to put it down
again,
whispered my thoughts outloud and swallowed
the pain.

I've never needed you as much as I do right now,
Doing everything I can to make you proud.
Living this life for us both, staying on my own
two feet,
bringing a little of you to everyone I meet.

But life is chaotic and loud and a mess,
You'd know what to do with this anxiety and
stress.
I can't come back home for a hug and some tea,
and for you to advise me and help me to see.

I've missed you a thousand times and a million
ways,
but never more than I do today.
I know you're around, keeping me right
and tomorrow won't be as dark as tonight.

Life can be cruel and mocking and rough,
and just when I feel like I've taken enough,
I remember although you're no longer here,
I have an angel for a mum and you're always
near.

Enough

Every once in a while, someone will stumble
upon you and your chaos and they'll stay.
Sometimes for a minute, sometimes forever and
sometimes no more than a day.

You'll get lessons and blessings and choices and
fun, memories and moments and magic.
And if it all ends there are multiple ways from a
conscious uncoupling to tragic.

The thing you must always remember though,
however the story unfolds,
is the power and beauty and sunshine and truth
you are enough- with or without someone to
hold.

Break

A million little pieces of who I am, what I've done, things I've felt and been through,
Lie scattered on the floor, shining and scattering light and shadows across the room.
I'm not sure what triggered this break, but the pieces are smaller now than they were before, microscopic kaleidoscope pieces sending rainbows and rainstorms of memories across the walls of what should feel like home, but no longer does.
I've been here a hundred times. Putting myself back together. Compiling little pieces of me, sorting, colour coding, arranging, discarding and assembling.
We go again, like a diamond painting now, not like the lego I'm used to.
I often wonder how small the pieces can become and I get caught up in the fascination of putting myself back together with pieces as small as a grain of sand.
But then I realise, in order for them to be so small, I'd have to break and shatter all over again, and that thought is enough to bring tears to my eyes and a deep and weary, but familiar, ache in my bones.

I'm good at putting myself back together through practise, years and years of repeated actions. It comforts me and saddens me in equal parts and I begin to wonder when I stopped being whole, when I ever was and if I ever will be again.

www.ingramcontent.com/pod-product-compliance
Lightning Source LLC
Chambersburg PA
CBHW061323140726
47998CB00007B/2525